Between the Lines

with

TRUTH

&

PURPOSE

Victoria Huggins Peurifoy
and
RuNett Nia Ebo

Index

This page left blank on purpose

Faith

I've Been Caught Up ✤

Once I lived my life believing the lie
that fortune and fame would lift me up high.
The higher I was lifted, the more my soul drifted
into the depths of evil till I thought I would die. But
now, I'm caught up and I've been shaken about.
God saw my misery and then, He snatched me out.
I've been touched by the Spirit.
I've been saved by His grace.
When you see me now, you
see a smile on my face.
Before when I had money, I was selfish and mean
People tried to talk to me, and I would make a scene
When I was broken, my sinful life was like mud.
Jesus came and saved me with His redeeming
blood. That's why, I'm caught up and I've been
shaken about. I was hurt and desperate and filled
with self-doubt.
I've been touched by the Spirit.
I've been saved by God's
Grace. That's why I can show
you a smile on my face.

It's Christmas

It's Christmas again, like a birthday that returns, to
be celebrated once more. Throughout the years,
people still shuffling and hustling to get that great
gift, not remembering what the purpose is, and
whose birthday it really is.

We celebrate the birth of Jesus, which was a
grand event. But his birth is an afterthought. I
wonder where it went. Folks going into debt,
to buy presents, forgetting the best present of
all, was the birth of Jesus Christ.

Maybe I should say, when you buy that next gift,
say to yourself, what would Jesus do or is that too
passé'? Let it snow, let it snow, let it snow, might
be the song you sing during your Christmas. Eve
of memories, but the three wise men managed to
get to Bethlehem so that they could bring gifts to
the baby who is the truth.

Merry Christmas to you, while you keep Jesus

as the reason for the season. When you sing
"I'm dreaming of a White Christmas", think of
the Virgin Mary and Joseph's struggle to bring
the King of Kings into this world.

A Soldier's Mantle ✵

On television, the hero saves the day.
He always got the enemy; in triumph;
then, he rode away.

The war movies showed him marching
for the right.
Marching headlong into battle until he
was out of sight.

The courageous soldiers blew up the foe
or caused them to retreat.
You seldom saw the TV soldier
stride off in defeat.

Townspeople welcomed soldiers who would save
them.
Cursing the enemy who economically enslaved them.

In reality, brave soldiers still fight for the worthy cause;
peace-lovers view them with disdain and media is void
with their applause.

He is a soldier, a peaceful man-of-war
following orders to the letter.
Paying with an arm, a leg, an eye, or his/her life;
clinging to faith that life gets better.

Some return home traumatized, broken.
Carrying wounds, the naked eye can't see.
Some acclimate to home life right away while
other comrades disconnect from life and
family.

On television, the soldier heard the accolades.
He came home and his high school band
saluted him with a parade.

In the real world, he still may win the war, but
the cause may change midstream, so now, he's
unaware just what he's fighting for.

Brave soldiers provide protection for citizens of the U.S.
After extensive training, donning military dress. With
fortitude and mettle to get the job effectively done and
hanging onto hope that victory can be won.
© November 2014 R.N.E.

Turbulence

Don't get sick in the turbulence.
Ride out the storm.
Through difficulties—ride and
Bide your time and you will
Get through the storm.

I will not suffer thy foot to be moved…(Psalm 121) Hold
on, wait through your fear.
Listen for God's words, God's voice.
Don't make others suffer in your
Anger, bitterness, or trial. Turbulence is
Always temporary.

Walk in the principle of God's words.
Then you will walk with God. Do not
Question God's test. He needs to
See what you will do during the storm.
Remember, "no weapon formed against
 you shall prosper." (Isaiah 54:17)
© May 5, 2019, VHP

God Can

God can

--Thaw cold hearts

--Open closed minds

--Revive dying relationships

--Heal broken spirits

--Save emotionally drowning souls

--Fix damaged bodies

God can.

---God does.

----Just Ask.

Only What You Do for Christ Will Last

Yes…you are gifted with
Many skills. Walking, talking,
shouting, praying, teaching, and
preaching. But yours gifts and talents
are designed to glorify the Lord.

Walk in God's will, study to build,
Pray for answers, meditate on his word,
Redeem yourself. Remember, even
nature stands up, listens to and
applauds God.

We often sing, "How great thou
art", but our actions do not reflect
the spirit of God in us, the power of
God through us, or the anointing of
God in us. We fail to recognize
God's grace and mercy for us.

The job we have, the car, the homes,
our children, the blessing we've
gained, and merciful healing are all

God. Our Christ-like actions should
all have Christ written on all of it.

Only the things that you do for
Christ will last.

© August 2017 VHP

No Spirit of Fear

"For God has not given us a spirit of fear but of power and of love and of a sound mind." 2nd Timothy 1:7 NKJV

Where He leads, we shall follow
without a spirit of fear.
God has made it clear; He is always near.

We don't have to be afraid in any man's sight.
Judgement is God's alone
We stand by His might. We walk in His light.

He promised never to leave us
nor forsake us. So,
there is no reason to let doubt overtake us.

When God gives us a
mission, we are not to be
afraid; no cause to be
dismayed, His work won't be
delayed.

We should move forward in faith
because the Father has said we are
fearfully and wonderfully made.
© November 22, 2008, R.N.E.

Alive 🦅

New York City, UK, California

and Italy, China and Illinois

coronavirus that is tied up in the snare.

Flatten the curve is the new swerve.

No masks, no gloves, or ventilators

To be found. Hospitals running out of

supplies and running out of time.

One thing we shouldn't do is be afraid

of the unknown because knowledge is

power over fear. Invisible armies

trying to find a cure, but ,over 6000 have

already died in Italy and they say

it'll be 12 to 18 months before they

find a cure.

Zoom, Amazon, and Coke

are making lots of money and

they plan to hire a lot more folks,

while restaurant workers are

losing their jobs steadily.

Attacks on Asians y'all, that's not

the answer and will not resolve

a thing. Churches are now streaming

because social distancing is a

mandatory directive. Better pray

harder than we ever have before.

Stimulus packages are a great idea,

if we won't be penalized at the end

of the year. Will college students

come back safe from spring break?

Politicians talking about forgiving

student loans. Who are they kidding?

You may not have to pay today,

but you sure 'nuff will have to pay later.

The virus comes from droplets, coughing,

or sneezing. Wearing that mask and those

gloves in public places, is your decision

but if you're not sick, there's no reason.

Staying in place could be safer to hold onto

the life that God has given you. National

guard's, I hope will not be deployed,

to fight and win us over in this current war.

It's time to love up our children, play some

board games at home. Play some chess,

Family feud, monopoly and more. Bring back

the thought that says, "a family that prays

together stays together."

It won't be as long as it's been if we keep

our heads to the sky and pray to the Father

in heaven, that we make it through this crisis

unscathed and definitely alive.

God will take care of you

Through every day, o'er all the way

He will take care of you

God will take care of you.

"God will take care of you" is a hymn written by Civilla Durfee
Martin (August 21, 1866 – March 9, 1948) was a Canadian American
writer of many religious hymns.

Heavy Duty Faith ✤

Faith is the belief we have
in a Higher Power
My Heavy-Duty Faith assures me
God arrives in my darkest hour.

Faith tells us God makes promises
we can count on Him to keep.
Heavy-Duty Faith means anything
God does will always be complete.

The Highest Power I
know tells me what to do;
shows me where to go.
I put my trust in an Awesome God
who lifts me when I'm low.

Heavy-Duty Faith, it can
be the size of a mustard
seed. It doesn't have to be
big, it just has to be deep.
God says that's all we need.   © March 29, 2021 R.N.E.

Moved to Tears 🐚

Moved to tears was my
response. "So great to hear your
voice you scared us, Girl."
"I love you,
please take care of yourself
"Oh my God. Thank God you're home.
"If you need someone to walk with you. I got you."
I called my family and friends after being released from
the hospital...
"Girl, everybody was praying for you.
"I tried to call you. I didn't know what happened.
I was scared."
"I am thankful that you are above ground."
Some people cried out loud and praised God on the
spot. Happy that I was doing better. I was moved to
tears as people expressed their heartfelt feelings about
me as a person, their loved one, their friend, their
neighbor, their ride-or-die, go-to

God had healed me. There was a pause in the atmosphere,
but I was moved to tears.   © April 2021, V.H.P.

24

Grief

Before I Die

1. As life appears each day, my thoughts are in an imaginative state of mind. Peace - represents quiet, contentment, a good book to read, a walk, a breeze, and a genuine companion to love.

2. I have never been one for mountain climbing, however, if you gave me a camera with telephoto lenses, along with a pen and pad, I would shoot every facet of the snowdrifts and caps, the foggy steam from invisible roads, hidden streams and even catch the sun on an angle to the left of the cliffs and lakes. A pen and pad would be used to scratch the pain that enhances the photographic descriptions.

3. Go to cities never visited. I'll ride on my imaginary red carpet. Hotel stays will be in an exquisite luxury suite, that exposes iconic columns that separate the living room from the dining area. There will be a teakwood spiraling staircase. It will lead to a boudoir which is adorned in ornate ivory brocade bedding and drapery. The furniture will be quality oakwood. The kitchen will be modern and

fully stocked with all my favorite fruits, vegetables, seafood, and real organic beverages will be for my delight.

4. Suddenly, in 2022, when I have turned 70, a book that I wrote a while ago, but was released in 2013, will hit the bestseller list, because someone affluent read it and called it a treasure. Though everyone who had already read it called it brave, fun, nerve-wracking... In a good way, a great read and exciting, because they knew me and realized I could be deep, but now the world knows it too. I have been a blade of grace in God's eyes, but every day, I have been blessed with many blades of grass. that are now a sprawling pasture for me to lie upon and relish the gloriousness of the Father.

5. A trip to Spain, maybe off the coast of the Canary Islands to see the underwater museum sculptures by John De'Clares Taylor. I will snorkel for the first time. I want to see the Museo Atlántico, it's part art and part artificial reef. Such fabulous pieces of art many will not see, but I will.

6. Long before I am ushered to my heavenly home, my first child's face, charm, whimsical stories, and the never

felt swaddling of his arms, will stop penetrating my silent anguish. A stare of endearment, a frontal lobe kiss, a bear hug will be given - - where release will never be wanted. My smile will never die.

© March 29, 2020, VHP

Black Angel ✿

He does not sing.

He does not want to rejoice

He is different from others in his midst.

He cannot lift his voice.

Even though he is with them,

He feels very alone

He should be happy.

He should like his new home.

Yet, this sad angel is in heaven alone.

What can he do? Where can he go?

He does not know. He does not know.

He walks around looking

Seeking a familiar face

But in this place,

It seems hopeless, and he cries.

He cries but men don't cry,

But he's not a man; not anymore.

He sees others. They are angels; his kind.

Still, they are unknown to him at the same time.

He should be happy.

He should like his new home

But this sad, Black angel is in heaven alone.

Will others come? If they don't, can he go?

He does not know. He does not know.

He should be happy, but he does not care.

No Black angels in heaven

So, how can he be there?

He should be happy.

He should like his new home

But this Black angel is in heaven all alone.

©1971/revised 2002, R.N.E. (When I was a little girl a teacher told me that "Black people don't get to go to heaven.")

Be Still

No one knows or understands the
turmoil or the pain a widower or
widow goes through.

The loss of your companion is
troubling. No words are correct that
are expressed in love.
For now, you are lost and alone.

Your Heavenly Father will contain the
grief, that's what you're always told. But
when you are consumed by your loss, it is
too compelling to control.

No constant date,
No shoulder nearby to lean upon,
No earthly comforter with you resides,
No lover to release your pain.
You cannot even describe, how lost sometimes you feel.

No one knows or cares to understand
the harshness of grief can be a drain. If
they knew, they would see the challenges
one experiences as sorrow tugs away. Folks
don't understand because they want to limit
your mourning timeframe.

Peace be still, my heart, please be still.
God, please control my anxiety,
please control my pain, please,
Father, squash the grief I feel, cuz
these folks down here, they don't
know or care to understand.
© March 27, 2020, V.H.P.

No Regrets

When the Good-bye Comes

When it's time to say that final good-bye, don't be
depressed, though you might want to cry. You
might struggle with what you want to say but
don't have a coulda', shoulda', woulda' day.

Don't talk about what you coulda' done
because you really did a lot.
When good things happened,
you gave Mom praise;
while some of the bad, you blamed on Pop.

Don't dwell on what you shoulda said
or words that remained unspoken.
The bonds of love whether strong or strained;
they can be bent but not broken.

Don't dwell on what blessings woulda come.
There were many that you shared.
The best blessing was being a part of their lives
and letting them know that you cared.

So, when the good-bye
comes and it's time to let go,
you won't have regrets
'though tears may flow.

No coulda, woulda, shoulda day for you.
Hold memories of your loved one tight.
Bid your loved one a sweet farewell as
they are led home by the Guiding Light.
© 2020, R.N.E.

Tired of Crying

I am angry and mad as hell.
Tired of crying, fearful of the unknown. No
longer is it just our men, now it is also our
women too, who are a part of the planned
executions. When will they leave us alone?

First our men were taken from their homeland-
mother Africa, then they were separated from
their families and brought.
to another land. A land that spoke a foreign language. This
place, unfamiliar, cold-hearted, distant place, they were
brought here to work on land that was not their own, so
Massa could get his fill.

His fill of all the skills and creativity
that were innately our own and used it and abused it
in the fields and in the home. We are the ones who
should be angry, angry for over 400 years of
mistreatment, misguidance, misappropriation of
funds...with no reparation in sight.

Even when you try to do things right, try

to do things better,

try to show more character, it doesn't matter, you

are still considered an animal, still considered

nothing, still not considered of value.

still not considered someone who feels

anything!

Each mother stands at the window looking at her

son leave for his destination, wondering

>   will he return?

>   Will I see my son again?

>   Will he look the same as when he left?

>   Will the wolves get him?

She wonders and then she prays,

>   "Lord, please take care of my child when he's away from
me...keep a hedge of protection all around him
Father. Amen."

Don't want to have to cry no more.

>   Don't want to have to feel that pain anymore.

>   Don't want to ask the question...Why?

I'm mad as hell right now and I'm ready to fight...
Understand please… I'm sick and tired of crying.

Rain

I always love rain at funerals. At least
when I'm outside, the raindrops
collide with the sadness so no one
can see me cry.

A deluge of emotions washes over me
when I'm sad. The showers outside
conceal the torrent of saltwater emerging
from my eyes.

When I don't completely wipe my face,
the dew from teardrops remains; just a
sprinkle of what used to be a flood.

Those other times when someone touches
my heart with sweet sentiments when there
is no sadness or death in the air, other
teardrops fall, and I embrace the liquid
sunshine.
© September 5, 2017 R.N.E.

I Won't Complain 🔆

(Dedicated to and speaking for my late husband who never

complained.)

Jesus, what I've been through with this

throat cancer does not compare to the

loving sacrifice that you made for me.

So, I won't complain.

Jesus, this smoking started all this

Reconstruction of the neck,

This stoma to breathe,

This fistula of corrosion, and

The skin graft that scars forever

I'm scarred, and frustrated. Scared,

But I won't complain.

Jesus, if you hadn't blessed man with skills,

I would not have survived this long.

I already said, I'm scared. I'm frustrated.

I've cried. I'm angry. Doggone it.

I'm P-Oed too! Oh, excuse me, Lord,

I was havin' a pity party, But,

I won't complain.

Live. Love. Hope. I have to
Keep hoping.
Keep praying
Keep believing
Keep being a blessing
Keep loving
Keep living And yes
Lord – I forgot I won't'
complain.

If I don't complain, no one will know My
real pain. No one will see how out of
control I feel. No one can change my life,
not even me. Jesus, thank you for loving
me.

Thank you for your grace. Thank you for life,
Thank you for my family, my doctors, and
Thank you for giving me strength so
I won't complain.
© 2008, V.H.P.

Mother Earth is Crying ❀

Mother Earth is crying. Blood has washed her feet
yet again. She has embraced another young soul.
They only had one life to live, and it was stolen.

Taken by one who did not believe
that heartbeats matter.
Mother Earth is in mourning.

So many seeds swallowed up by violence
before they had a chance to really
sprout. Barely got their feet wet when
someone decided to end their cycle.

Sorrow and Heartache knocked on Mother
Earth's door and placed yet another
lifeless, pre-mature adult
in her arms.

© June 2, 2017, R.N.E.

41

The Voice that Used to Talk to Me.

(Dedicated to my late husband, who lost his voice to Throat Cancer)

It is said that "Silence is golden," but as I watched the TV, I asked questions to which only you would have the answer. And then it hit me when you didn't respond…. You can no longer talk to me.

You are the historian in the family, and you could discuss lost dynasties, art history and what year an event took place…then it hit me. Your voice can longer talk to me.

Even when you want to fuss at me, my heart winces at the sight of your mouth moving, brow frowning, and your hands railing in the air…Your voice no longer fusses at me.

I cry in my sleep when I think of the debates, the laughter, The private conversations that won't happen with your voice anymore. No longer can the voice that God gave you…talk to me.

When we married, you told the world that communication would be the nucleus of our survival, and then all this stuff happened. I now want what I cannot have – the voice that used to talk to me.

Grandmom Has a Hole in Her Heart

She opens her arms but no little
one will fill them no little feet
will run to her no tender voice
to tickle her ear.
When mommy and daddy's love fell apart
Grandmom was left with a hole in her heart.

She rocks in her chair staring at
a picture frame; a frame of
memories gone by memories of
her little Sugar Pie, the one true
apple of her eye but thoughts
of her now, make Grandmama
cry.

She opens her arms, when she closes
them again there's nothing there but
empty space. No bright eyes gazing
up from a handsome little face.
No voice to say

"Love you, Grandmama dear."
Words that Grandma loved to hear.

When mommy and daddy's love fell apart
Grandmom was left with a hole in her heart.

Grandmama misses telling stories
to the little one who sat on her lap.
Weekend and holiday visits are no more.
Her little grandchild won't be back.
No more embraces; Grandmama is missing
the precious one that she loved kissing.

Since the parents were always
fighting, Mom took the baby and
departed.
Dad, left in pain; would never be the
same but Grandmama; no one saw
that she was brokenhearted.
© January 13, 2013 R.N.E.

This page left blank on purpose

First Love ✼

Youth is a wonderful time to experience first love.
There is a tenderness that makes it fragile.
Your feelings are all over the place.

The giddiness, the butterflies, the queasiness in
the pit of your stomach when you can't speak
while face to face. The yearning when you haven't
spoken for days. Absence making the heart grow
anxious.

Being close creates a flame.
It burns bright with passion and flickers in
awkward moments. There is an enchantment to
young love; that virgin encounter, unblemished
by residue of previous hurts. Those haven't
happened yet. All the more reason to relish that
first love.
© June 2017, R.N.E.

Joy This Way

Like you, I get excited, for
each communication
I receive. Wondering

what things are delighting you
and how you are feeling as
you dream.

Sheltering in place has its benefits, but
I haven't found one yet
I feel cooped up in an indecisive

mode as to what I will do next.
There is plenty to be done around
the house, but my interest

Levels just aren't there, but they
spike when I think of you.
It won't be as long as it has been,

that's what I keep telling myself.

Oh boy, you just wait until the iron gates of
life magically open themselves.

Keep telling myself, don't get yourself
Excited, keep your shield up at all costs.
I think the shield has a crack in it and

it's causing me to get lost. Lost
in my thoughts of you making
me smile all day

it's such a nice feeling to be
receiving attention and Joy
this way.
© March 29, 2020 V.H.P.

Familiar Heartbeat ✵

Fascinated, but not intrigued.
Yet something about you made me smile.
Our eyes connected; you touched my hand.
My heart went completely wild.

You won me over; became my solace.
The one I looked for; you were my "home."
The voice that soothed me when we danced
close.
Your heartbeat was my comfort zone.

I ran to you when bullies stressed
me; when I hurt or jobs depressed
me. My head on your shoulder, my
hand on your chest.
The rhythm of your heart put my worries to rest.

I sought you when daily stuff got too tough
or gave me the blues
or times when I was stretched thin, at a
breaking point or felt abused.

You were my haven here on land
the next best thing to holding God's hand.
Your heartbeat set a steady pace for me...
Now all I have left is the memory
©October 2017. R.N.E.

Great Grandmom

It is 1945. She hums a song. It is too late
For a demure woman to have More
children of her own.
Yet, she is forever surrounded
By children, who are not hers
Biologically, but still belong to her.

Time has not been kind.
Her hands are what people remember.
They were soft from many years of
Cocoa butter love. But she always sits
In the same spot every day, with a lap
That shelters hands that have been
Arthritically ravaged. Her wooden porch And
familiar rocking chair are like a photo Of art
of Great Grandmom.

The world is escaping her sight.
Sunflowers, lilac, and lavender aromas
Bring peace. Then her senses are distracted
By children's voices -

"Get from over there," she musters a yell.
Children - great-grandmom loves them,

    "Old people cannot raise these fast youngsters," She
often would say.
    "It's too much, too wearing, too
time consuming on the spirit.
She would declare.

She was a gentle soul, kind, and soft-spoken.
Her smile and her voice could melt a child's heart.
Great-Grandmom, her memory is all we have
Her humming said, "Home."
© October 7, 2019, VHP

Hot Ice �֍

When we met your heart was
wrapped in an igloo with a
Do Not Enter sign on the door.

I was the pursuer being chased by
the part of you that wanted to be captured.
To touch you meant being burned
by ice that froze my desire to flee.

You held me.
I felt my doubt melting

while a cool blue blaze of trust

sparked within me.

To be with you meant going through
an avalanche of emotions
from icy hot to smoldering cold.
When the frosty smoke enveloped me, I
knew you were in the middle of a thaw.

© September 13., 2006, R.N.E.

We Were at it Again

Once more, we're at it again. Loving, musing, fussing,

arguing, and making love again. We feed on

each other's intelligence,

 each other's heart strings,

  each other's funny bone,

   each other's dancing the bump,

    each other's poetry, and

     each other's ways of being alive.

Yet, we are here, at it again, or should I say,

he was at it again, getting up under my skin

with the drugs, drinking his life away,

smoking his weed with asthmatic nostrils

which had a hold on him. It was all extreme to me.

He was different, he wasn't the same person

that I used to know and play games with—

before he went to Vietnam.

I didn't smoke, do drugs, or drink,

or intentionally waste my time-- except on him.

His hold on me was the bat he loved to swing

and the constant rhythm with which I purred.

He had a hold on me, like the spiraling

structure of DNA with its double helix of

genetic information, except,

we were not related. There were times

when we were like the original Pangaea,

the supercontinent. However, there was

an opening of the San Andreas fault-

which was our relationship. Our very togetherness

just cracked and separated us like a concrete split –

we were working on parting ways—but

he did not know it yet.

I wrote a 10-page, two-sided, legal pad letter saying,

"I'm tired of the manic craziness that is your world."

He had only one question,

"Do you mean we can't try again?"

"Yes" I said, "We cannot try again."

Therefore, we will not be at it once again,

at least, not until the next time.

© October 22, 2019, VHP

Slow Progression ✤

There are times when you rush
my senses like a soft breeze
picking up momentum to
become intoxicating until eating,
thinking, and speaking blend
together.
Sleeping becomes impossible and
I am a major emotional mess.
There are times when your image
drifts into my thoughts   s-l-o-o-o-w-l-y
like soft clouds on a warm day.

The dynamics of a complex plan,
I've been working on for months
take a backseat to your smile.

There are those times when you can
be as mean as a fire-breathing dragon
on a rampage and God help me,
I still want you. B-A-A-A-D!
©October 10. 2004, R.N.E.

The Voice

Why does your voice make me smile?
The intonation, ebbs and flow are new
and exciting. I barely recall such a voice.
I hear who you were and who you are now.
A Child of God who recognizes his
Faults and to whom he must answer. God, I
just want to know if this time in my life Is the
answer to a long prayer.
© December 16, 2020, VHP

Chained to Me ❁

Chained to me,
something you were not ordained
to be but you remained with me
while this cancer was nothing
but a pain to me.
It was plain to see how this disease
was gradually stealing life from me.

Grateful to you that fateful day I got
the news. You were faithful
while I acted in a way that was so
hateful to you; you were graceful
and true despite everything I put you
through.
Now, I'm regretting all the drama
that I hurled at you.

Shameful of me
I made you the target of grief
that slowly enveloped me.

Truly that was not how things
between us were supposed to
be.

You chose to be the rock
that I needed desperately
in the hour of distress when
my future seemed to be
a question mark.

Chained to me though you never
did make effort to explain to me
why you remained with me
when all I did was treat you
badly.

Yet, when my depression lifted
it soon came to me that this was
the worse that it could ever be.
Through thick and thin; good
times out or bad times in,
no matter what rides on the
wind, I love you madly.
© March 26, 2018, R.N.E.

Poetry is (An Anaphora poem)

Poetry is my reason to dream.

Poetry is a melody of thoughts.

Poetry understands me.

Poetry is my way of examining the world, even when my reactions are delayed.

Poetry is the tune sung while jumping Double Dutch.

Poetry is a character that lives inside of me.

Poetry is quality time thinking.

Poetry is a visit to the galaxies of love

Poetry is a way to escape when no one gets me.

Poetry is my turquoise water bottle.

Poetry is my first love; it is in the voice of my heart.

Poetry is a thorn that pricks my side and is a force that writes a special line.

Poetry pushes me when I'm trying to give up.

Poetry never times me, stops me, judges me, slaps me, or even tells me off.

Poetry loves who I have become.

Poetry has a mind of its own. It makes me write poems I didn't plan to write.

Poetry makes me say things I didn't know I was thinking.

Poetry turns me inside out and hums in my ears.

Poetry is a fancy way of breaking the rules.

Poetry is the fabric of my inner most desires.

© May 2, 2017, VHP

This page left blank on purpose

Desperate Times

Hello Tomorrow, I Need You

Hello Tomorrow,
I know you're coming.
You aren't here yet, but I need you.
I need you because my today is
confusion, and my yesterdays are broken.

Broken because of all the pain and hurt
they possess. My yesterdays hold the
sadness of loved ones gone;
some by their own hands.

Hands that used to touch me and
show me they loved me but now, mine
are the ones that are empty. Some of my
yesterday's grip sorrow and regret
so tight I can't even remember
what my dreams look like.

I miss the yesterdays filled with hope
that sparked a flame in my life
and made my future look bright.
Tomorrow, I need you so much.

Today, I'm stuck in limbo.

Moving left or right seems impossible.

My vision is clouded by pain.

But Tomorrow,

you have always been

pregnant with possibilities.

Some of them quite unthinkable

until they are birthed.

I need you to help me bear down

and push out my future.

Be my labor coach,

Tomorrow.

Hold my hand and tell me to

"Breathe."

© December 2016 R.N.E.

The Sisters Three

Oh, I have body parts all interesting in their special way. but the sisters three get my attention more than I would like...you see it's their way. They are meteorologists and are accurate every time. They ignore walking canes when they call out to them to assist. To the sisters, canes are a waste of time.

The sister's three have the initials S. S. and H., almost like the S&H food stamps from back in the day. Anyway, these sisters have no sympathy, empathy, or compassion to spare or share. I have body parts that are interesting in their own special way.

Let me introduce you to sisters, spinal stenosis, sciatica, and herniated disc. They have conferences calls about how much they plan to hurt me. You see that snowstorm we had this winter; I knew about it three days before it came. The sisters three told me in their own special weather report called pain. In the process, they brutally beat me up along the way. I need to trade them in. Do I have any takers today?

© February 7, 2021, V.H.P.

The Streets Can't Have My Son

No son of mine will study Thug-

ology when he's only seven.

No one's putting a gun in his hand to

take a life at eleven.

Becoming much too hard and

cold.

Forgetting how to be young, acting

way too old.

Don't want mean to be his middle name or

him disrespecting women in his life.

Don't want him growing up using the B-

word or believing it's okay to beat his wife.

My son's not walking with his pants down

acting like the world should kiss his butt,

and even if she chooses to act like one;

I'll not be the mother who raises a son

to treat any girl he meets like a slut.

Becoming much too hard, too

cold; Deleting his youth going too

fast to old.

No, the streets can't have my son.

Four-letter words won't define his life.

He has to set goals, have ambition and

drive

and by God's grace; maybe he'll stay alive.

Whether he dresses in a suit and tie, casual

wear or sweats;

he will be clean and respectful,

living his life with fewer regrets.

Sorry, the streets can't have my son.

I'm teaching him what's wrong and what's

right.

The streets may try to take him or even try to

break him but they can't have my son…

no, they won't get my son.

The streets can't have my son without a fight!

© March 21, 2021, R.N.E.

Collateral Damage

We are but collateral damage.
Coronavirus understands its
Objective. Seek, find, and destroy.
Lamenting about what hasn't been done,
Lends itself to a waste of time.
Advice given attracts deaf ears.
Taking us to a terroristic level.
Examine the players who
Reel us in, with their constant barrage of
Assaults of doom and
Litany of, "it is what it is."

We are but collateral damage.
Destroy the people and saturate their minds.
Angle your temperature guns at their heads,
Managing in the process, to get them prepared…for the
end Ask the man no questions, for we already know
Guns, conspiracies, and fudging is the way to go.
Elections are coming, the fix is already in the mix

We are but collateral damage.

    We are but collateral damage

You must know it is *what it is*,

But we can change what it ain't.

© April 15, 2020, VHP

Missing in Action

Blood and tears litter the streets where I live
More mothers are childless today.
More young people are M.I.A.
Missing in Action at school.

His voice won't ask the hard questions in History.
Why he had to die; that's now the mystery.
This student is the history lesson today.
The 2-hundredth-something child
to lose the breath of life.

Missing in Action at play.
One less basketball bouncing through hoops.
Nothing but net. Nothing, but net.

The ball won't be traveling across concrete,
or under the arms of two young sons.
Young ones with dreams of the NBA
Dreams in one millisecond gone away.
One took a gun, shot the other.
It's hard to believe that they were like brothers.

No longer strangers to hurt, harm and danger.
Statistics now. One got life; the other has none.

Missing in Action at home.
The jump rope sits abandoned in the corner.
The girl's leg hurts from the bullet
that crossed her door.
She wasn't even jumping at the time.
Wasn't reciting her favorite rhymes while
trying to raise her score.
She was just sitting on the floor.

Watching cartoons when the bullet said
"hello." For her to walk, that piece of metal
had to stay.
Now all she wants is the pain to go away.

Residents of Lost Souls Cemetery.
Neighbors living on Crushed Dreams Drive.
Inhabitants of Stolen Futures Lane.
Hope strained. Aspirations drained.
Emptiness for some is all that remains.
Missing in Action.
©2006, R.N.E.

Not One Gun

As he wheels his rifle freely in the breeze the Popo treat

him kindly and let him walk with ease. For a brother the

outcome would not have been the same. He would be dead

in the street or been badly maimed.

Injustice right in front of us for the
whole world to view, but they don't see
the problem it's all about the hue. It's so
blatant and so hurtful it's all about who's
viewing this disparity about arms. Look
what happens if a white boy wheels a
rifle at everyone, and a black boy has
chewing gum.

I wish the roles could be reversed in
this unfair and inequitable land. So
other folks would understand it's
not the magician's sleight of hand
but the evilness of man.

(poem about Kyle Rittenhouse) © August 31, 2020 V.H.P.

Desperate Times �֍

Lord, Deliver me from evil.
My life is in upheaval
as I take time to pray
that You repair my disarray.
I know I should simply wait on You.

You who sit high and look low.
Tell me where I should go
because only You know
what's supposed to happen next.

For Thine is the kingdom,
the power and the glory,
reflecting on the story of all
that You have done

How You offered up Your Son
for all of us troubled ones
still trying to find our way.
This is why we pray.

You are All-mighty, -powerful,
mercy-full and full of grace.

Help me to fill this space
where I feel nothing lives.

Show me where I belong,
for I long to be whatever You see in me
because I know the me, I see has limits.

These are desperate times with critical places
filled with many wearing intense faces
not wanting to be judged
as they find out who they are.

Some heap judgment on others,
pointing fingers at their sisters and brothers;
disregarding that inevitably
Thy Will, will be done.
No doubt, when Thy kingdom comes
all will be stunned!

© April 18, 2016, RNE

Being Seen 🦢

Being seen during the pandemic,
Humm, opportunities few and far between.
Our cars sat in place, as if at attention.
Nothing was open, nowhere to go.
Unless food shopping, or toilet paper buying
Was your thing, you know.

Being seen during the pandemic
Was impossible, at least if you were
Used to performing on stage. No more
Audiences to cheer you on, no more traffic
Jams to give you pause. No sir, during the
Pandemic, activities were unallowed.

Being seen during the pandemic was
Not necessary. You were either working from home,
Home schooling your children, cleaning out your
Basement, getting rid of clothes, getting to know
Your children, playing board games, watching TV
Together, or sitting somewhere--bore out of your gourd.

Being seen was not something many senior citizens
Desired to do. Hemmed up in their homes, even their
children could not be seen. Thank God for Google Duo,
Facetime, And other social media platforms. For an entire
year, hugging was off limits, I think I missed that the most.
But one thing for sure, we became more paranoid, and
afraid to go out of doors.

Being seen during the pandemic was a
Virtual tour to the doctor's office, a zoom trip
Through your laptop, a desire to just be with
Family, friends, and close associates.
Isn't it funny, the things we missed when we were
Forced to stop--being seen?

© May 4, 202,VHP

This page left blank on purpose

IJS

I'm Just Saying

Beauty Affirmed �֍

I see young women,
my young, ebony sisters hiding under wigs
cloaked under pricey weaves.
Buried under "other people's hair."
Making people who don't look like them rich!

"Is that hair yours?"
"Sure is! I paid for it. Paid with hard earned
money. Paid for it sitting for hours while
somebody pulled, sewed, wove and glued it to me.
Paid for it by "sleeping cute"
and sacrificing plenty of good lovin.'
Telling him he better not touch. It hasn't set
yet."
Maybe they don't want to Go Natural like I did.
So be it; but it stings in my heart when some
don't see their true beauty.
A few think the Afro was a hair-do, a 70's style,
just to be worn for the disco scene.
That myth started by those who wouldn't wear it
and repeated by the ones who see it as un-done.

But we, who wear it have reclaimed ourselves,
embracing our tight curls. Remembering

what Dr. Maya said, "Rugs have naps."
I just have very, curly hair, naturally!
This on my head is real and its mine.
Yeah, I know someone made a song-
I am not my hair. Good for her.
As for me, I am my hair, my lips, my hips and more.
Different looks evoke different attitudes.
Variety is good but so is being true to self.
I embrace all that God gave me, all that God made me.
He did not lie. I am beautiful because I am His.
An' if you don't think so
You jus' need glasses!

Dragon Voice

My voice is my dragon,
full of fire and force. The
tongue is my dragon
whose filter is lost.
Lost in making good choices
there's a penalty to pay.
Impatience is my dragon, it
keeps me waiting for a prayer
to be answered. The voice of
understanding is a dragon that
does not exist according to
entitled people. I am the
dragon big and strong watch
me roar all night long.
Roaring out truths that no one
Wants to hear. My dragon
Voice is something to fear.
May catch you right, may catch
You wrong. Just be prepared, For what
the dragon voice will bring on.
© 5/2/2019, V.H.P.

Faded Friendly Blue

At school, one day when I was
young, a man in blue came to
our class.
Teacher said, "This is Officer Smith.
Officer Smith is your friend.

If you get lost, find him.
He can help you get home.
He can help you find your
puppy if it strays.

If someone is chasing you,
he can make them stop."
But who finds Officer Smith
when he's lost in the madness of his
own demons?

Who stops Officer Smith when she
forgets she's supposed to protect
and serve?

Who restrains Officer Smith when
his arrested development
releases the PTSD monster that
swallowed his human heart
so that Black lives only matter
horizontal in a body bag?

When I was in first grade a man in
blue came to our class. By the time
I reached sixth grade,
he'd made his quota.

© June 6. 22019 R.N.E.

Blue Lights

As I sat in my hospital bed, there was nothing to do. I contemplated the possibilities of making up something that was new. No television to watch, no phone to speak on, not even a cell phone nearby to distract me from my situation. So, I focused on the TV screen which had a blue image, that had a fence in front of it. The scene never changed. It was just a psychedelic looking picture with only colors of blue and white swirling all around. However, the creative side of my brain went a little haywire. I decided I was going to see if I could pull any images out of what appeared to be nothing. After much concentration, I did find the image of a baby in utero, a Maverick, the profile of a man, a German shepherd's sleeping face, and a tree. There, I did it and I sat down and wrote a poem about it.

Blue Lights Poem

The profile of a man may tell you
many things. He is strong, he is
funny, he is mean, or his character is
flawed, or perhaps he is sweet as
sugar and cream.

The Maverick, wild and free,

uninhibited by restrictions, fearless,

and brave. Not much open space

for him to run free now.

As a baby in utero floats, he has the

comfort of his mother's heartbeat,

instantaneous food, warmth, and an

instant swimming pool.

The sleeping dog should not be disturbed.

He may be dreaming, and he should be

allowed to stay that way or there will be hell,

to pay. The tree of life, that could have

sustained us all, was put to rest at man's fall.

© March 1, 2020

Guilty Until Proven ❦

My crime is not my name
but the real shame is
whenever things go wrong
I'm the first to get the blame.

Why did you point your finger here?
I thought I made it clear that the
foolish me from long ago is not the
man you've come to know.

I've given you no reason
to come and accuse me
but you and others find it
far too easy to abuse me.

It does not amuse me that
you think my crime made
me a criminal forever.

Too many think I should be
the scapegoat for their trouble.

I hate to bust their bubble but
this time, the fault's not mine.

I served my time. I paid my dues.
Believe me or not; you have to choose.
Who I am now,
is not the person I was then
and you could accept that
if you really were my friend.
© July 23, 2018, R.N.E.

To Jail – A Golden Shovel

This world is fractured. **Trying**

to heal from loneliness and non-connections, **so the**

belligerence of people has gone buck wild. It is **hard**

to feel golden in your spirit, when, **to**

find clarity, it is cloudy at best. We **put**

up with certain renditions of justice. But then **the**

compassion and forgiveness that folks used to have is **bad**

news now, it doesn't exist. Non-conviction of the **guys**

known as police, who killed Brianna Taylor, **in**

her sleeping bed, should not be reinstated, in **jail.**

they should go,

© September 24, 2020. V.H.P.

91

Reporting for Duty

Mother Nature dealt a mega-ugly hand
many found hard to believe or understand
the what, the when, the who and the why
but people all over the world began to die.

Like a raging tornado, the rampant killer came
taking down one person, then another, then
more famous or average, it did not matter;
your father, mother your sister, or brother.
Soon all beds were full on the hospitals' floors.

They called this virus Covid-19 because
in 2019 it introduced itself.
First Responders rolled up their sleeves
ready to mete out the hand we all
were dealt.

Tirelessly, endlessly working 24-7.
Deciding it best not to go home.
Taking precautions with loved ones;
compassionate to strangers, stationed
by their bedside so they were not alone.

Doctors, Nurses, other medical staff;
round the clock duty but patients kept
coming. Some asymptomatic, others far more
dramatic.
Up and down the corridors, ventilators humming.

Firefighters, paramedics, some city workers on
call; suddenly storekeepers are essential workers
too.
Police maintaining order, security watching out
for hoarders. To mask or not to mask?
People not sure what to do.

Businesses shutdown. Families on lockdown.
Students, all levels learning remotely.
Workers kept trying but co-workers were
dying as others experience PTSD.

To all the workers and many others who helped
during this crisis that could have torn our universe
apart;
we honor and respect you and we will not forget
you. You deserve applause and a velvet purple heart.
© March 2021, R.N.E

Entitlement Certification 宅

To achieve this entitlement certification, It is
necessary for you to be self-centered, always
focused on what you get out of the deal, not
concerned with how other people may be
affected, you must feel it's your own privilege
to receive the certification and no special work
is required for you to get what you want in
life. You need not aspire to be anything and
you must expect that everything will be
handed to you on a silver platter.

Should you be selected for this auspicious
certification, you must wear this document on
your back at all times, so that people will know
how hard you have worked. In addition, you
must provide 50 hours of community service at
a homeless shelter, a soup kitchen, or any other
place where people are in need. After these
50 hours, your certification will be validated
by the state   that you live in.
© April 2021, VHP

Bullet-Proof Living ✽

Bullet-proof living, invincible ones,
Believing they cannot be cut down by
guns.
Bullet-proof lives on borrowed
time;
not caring who they hurt when they
commit their crime.

Shootings, stabbings, a beat-down
now and then.
Doctors fix. Courts release.
Then it begins again.

Bullet-proof living. Dancing with danger.
Canceling the lives of friends and perfect strangers.
Bullet-proof lives? That's just a fairy tale
There are only three conclusions, dead,
maimed or locked in jail.
© April.14, 2014 R.N.E.

Her Name is... 🈂

In 1999 I met this lady and when I met her, she encouraged me to write a book even though she didn't know me, she sensed something in my spirit. She encouraged me to do something that I had always been told I should do...write.

I never saw her again until 2007, the year that I retired from the government. It turned out that God had a plan for the two of us. I had begun writing poetry, and had already published my first book, when I ran into her again at a poetry festival, we exchanged phone numbers and she subsequently took me under her wings.

She became my mentor, my friend, my sister from another mother, my shoulder to lean on, my confidant, and my Partner in Rhyme. One day, she presented me with an honor. She invited me to be her partner for her bi-monthly poetry event Poetify: Poetry to Edify.

God has a way of bringing people into your life who share some of your same situations, same joys, same pains, and who can tell when you are struggling emotionally, and can be a prayer warrior over you, and even love you when you're mothering her.

This lady that I'm speaking of is an honoree in her own right. We have had so many parallels and experiences within our lives, that sometimes, we even wear the same colors and earrings without calling one another. Sometimes when we go out and are performing together, or someone just sees us together, they will say,

"you two cannot deny that you are sisters." Biologically we may not be sisters, however, sisters in Christ we will always be. Her name is Runett Nia Ebo Gray…she is my muse. All accolade you receive, you deserve Sis. .

© January 2021, V.H.P.

Truth Beyond the Covers ✤

One late summer afternoon while I was pondering
sleep, some books in my library decided they had to
speak. So, I LET THE AXIOM SPEAK though I was
not so inclined because when the books started talking it
felt like *The Day I Lost My Mind*. I had to *Listen to The
Cries* of *a Man of Color* and witness *Women of Color*
shedding *Tears of Joy*.

But the tears become mor199363e salty when *A Memory
Forgotten* is the stinging one that sets in when they've lost
their growing boy. ADOPTION PANTOUN
opened its cover and I asked myself why a *Five-
Pound Bag of Sugar* could ever make me cry. *The
Answer was in Her Face* and soon in mine too as that
bundle of sugar invoked *Thoughts of You, Son*.
IN THE SPIRIT OF MY REMEMBERANCE,
the *Best Thing That Ever Happened* was the *Amazing Grace*
that God bestowed when He put this *Gentle Soul* in my
space.

She knows how to get a *Prayer* through while I think *No
One Understands*. When I think none can solve my
problems, she reminds me, "Yes, God can."

If I need her, she says, *"I'm Coming."* That's how I know
Angels Fly. It's ALL ABOUT THE WOMEN like that; all
about the ones who try. In the midst of their own troubles,
these women are ride-or-die. While suffering on uneven
roads of life, I know I am not alone. *"Can You See My Skid
Marks?"* She'll ask; then, show me her own. The marks on
A Woman's Back reveal burdens and laboring pain; just as a
Blade of Grace can pierce through the ground women who
want to, rise again. When *It's All About the Men* and time
for that book to talk to me, it told me that honest Black
men were about to make history. *In My Lifetime I Never
Thought* a man of color would be *The Voice that Used to Talk
to Me* so I'd find my identity. The speeches of Malcolm X
and Dr. Martin Luther King taught me not to let others
put me in *The Box* of how they see beauty. There is no
Remote Control that will manipulate my intelligence, my
culture or what I appreciate. There's *No Expiration Date* on
true friendship or dreams.

She taught me how to *Live, Love and Hope* 'til I split my
seams! I listen when *God's Calling*, yet I still wonder *Will I
Know* what God requires me to do in order to learn and
grow. But I won't let fear *Grip Me* because I *Remember Our
Talk* so when I sense evil in the air, I'll know it's time to
take a walk. Her books say the right *Attitude Has No Age;*

I'm a Defender of Truth as I take the world's stage. My purpose? Be inspired by God, revealing *Truth,* and spreading Joy, gaining knowledge from books written by Victoria "The Axiom" Peurifoy.

The titles of her poem book are featured in *Italics*.

Straight into the Nut House –

Reversed Golden Shovel 宅

I long to show the world what it

took to make me a real writer;.

you know, a real - lived a life - true soul

in every sense of the word.

As I create and revise verbiage there's

an ideal movie script within. The punchline is the

antidote to resolve the writer and

free them from - stuck mode - to a prompt

card that opens their world to possibilities,

out-sourcing ways to garner the right phrase

of emotions, action, or an object that releases

jail locks of complacency, humdrum lines,

and the blockage of thoughts that leads

straight to non-creativity. Let's go

into our memory banks and realize

the real answers that cause us to eat a

nut or two, have a wealth of memories in a

house called, "just start writing "and you too can

become real.

Contributors to **Straight into the Nut House**

Keesh, "I took you in as an antidote.'

and Chandra AKA Muffy "free card out of jail and straight

into the nut House"

@May 10, 2020, VHP

Bio's

RuNett Nia Ebo, Poet of Purpose, has been writing for more than 6 decades. She has self-published 8 chapbooks and 4 paperbacks of poetry, a CD, and a fiction story. Her work is in several anthologies including *The Storm Within* ©2002, *Stand Our Ground* © 2013 and *Seniors Rockin' the Pen* © 2014. The following year, (Feb 2015), RuNett and Victoria "The Axiom" Peurifoy, her Partner-In-Rhyme, released a poetry book they co-authored entitled *Truth with Purpose* © 2014. Her signature poem is "*Lord, Why Did You Make Me Black?*"©1994. It is featured in the newly released *Philly Jawn, for Women Revisited* ©2020, *Chicken Soup for the African American Soul* ©2004. It has also been written as a play and a children's version is now available as a coloring book.

Because of all the plagiarism of this poem, she has been dubbed "the Most Bootlegged Poet in Philadelphia."

She has performed her poems in various cities all over the country and in the Virgin Islands. She has appeared on cable and public television and been featured, or guest hosted on cable and regular radio programs. She has also participated in programs at The Clef Club, Freedom Theatre, Fresh Visions Youth Theater, and The African American Museum.

Ms. Ebo has visited schools (all grades) as part of "Nia's Purpose: Poetry & Percussion at Work." She is a recipient of the Golden Mic Award (2014) from World Renowned Entertainment and was honored for Poetic Excellence by Poetic Ventures and the National Black Authors' Tour (2016). Ms. Ebo has written 3 plays; one was inspired by her signature poem. She co-hosts "POET-IFY: Poetry to Edify" a bi-monthly poetry venue. **She is a contributing writer for Kwee, a Liberian magazine published in Monrovia and a blog- Keeping It Real, for her church's** website www.gcob1723.com. This author can be contacted via her website www.poetebo.com

BESE SAKA

"sack of cola nuts"

symbol of affluence, power, abundance, plenty, togetherness, and unity. The cola nut played an important role in the economic life of Ghana. A widely used cash crop, it is closely associated with affluence and abundance. This symbol also represents the role of agriculture and trade in bringing peoples together.

This symbol is used for Runett Nia Ebo's poetry. Nia means purpose and the purpose of her poetry is messages that pull people together.

http://www.adinkra.org/htmls/adinkra_index.htm

Victoria Huggins Peurifoy, also known as the Axiom, for she tells the truth, has authored 3 Chapbooks, 2 CDs, 7 poetry books, 1 autobiography, 1 memoir, 1 children's book, and 1 Medical Narrative. She is a contributor to 6 anthologies, co-authored 1 book with her Partner-in-Rhyme, Runett Nia Ebo and was ghost writer for 4 Senior Citizens. One of her signature poems, *Blackberry Love* was featured in a recent publication of

Philly Jawn – 20-+20 Women Revisited ©2020, Anthology #7 by Drexel University's Writer's Room © 2021, and. Victoria is a contributing author/poet to Philadelphia Moonstone Poetry's 2021 anthologies called This *Can't Happen Her and Haikus.* She recently published a new book entitled *The Triumph Continues*, which a sequel to *The Triumph Continues - A Medical Narrative.* She is a Writer in Residence with the Writer's Room of Drexel University and is also a member of the Canon Tripod Team which is a writer's room initiative. One of Victoria's photos was made into a mural which covers a wall in MacAlister Hall on Drexel's Campus. Victoria is the Facilitator for the Poetry and Discussion group and Co-Facilitator of The

Best Day of My Life (So Far) a story writing group at the Center in the Park's older adult center; located in Germantown. She co-hosts a bi – monthly poetry event called Poetify – Poetry to Edify.

Victoria is a senior citizen who has returned to school to complete her bachelor's degree in Organizational Leadership at Peirce College. She lives and breathes through the gift that God have given her—writing. In addition, Victoria is an active member of her church. She sings on the Church Chapel Choir and is a lead soloist, is a member of the Announcement Clerks, is a member of the Good Shepard Circle, and the Sheepfold of Peter Daniel at the White Rock Baptist Church in Philadelphia. Reach her for bookings at theaxiomsbooks@gmail.com or go to her website to order books at http://www.lulu.com/spotlight/vhp

GYE NYAME

"except for God" symbol of

the supremacy of God

This unique and beautiful symbol is ubiquitous in Ghana. It is by far the most popular for use in decoration, a reflection on the deeply religious character of the Ghanaian people.

This symbol is used for Victoria Huggins Peurifoy's poems for she represents the axiom which means truth and God is truth.

Victoria Huggins Peurifoy

Paperback

The Triumph Continues – A Covid Story & Poems ©2021

Triumph in Crisis – A Medical Narrative ©2017

Peace like a Stream – Poetry © 2017

A Journey in Life's Episodes Memoir ©2017

Co-Authored book: Truth with Purpose ©2014

Run Between the Raindrops ©2013

A Blade of Grace (Hardcover)Autobiography ©2013

A Blade of Grace (Soft cover)Autobiography ©2013

God's Calling - Poetry ©2012

Battery Man – Children's book ©2013

Let the Axiom Speak - Poetry ©2010

I Did Not Live in Vain – Biography-Ms. Cunningham

In the Spring of my Remembrance-Poetry

No Expiration Date - Poetry for Caregivers

The Wild Spirit Behind the Voice-Poetry ©2007

Chapbooks

There's a Story Here - Biography ©2013

Adoption Pantoum - Poetry ©2012

It's All About the Men Folks

CDs

Run Between the Raindrops & Let that Black
Man Walk

RuNett Nia Ebo ✤

Paperback

Poetry Has Raised Me © 2012

Poems of Nia book2 © 2011

God Has All You Need © 1996

Lord, Why Did You Make Me Black? - **coloring book** ©2018

Chapbooks-

Expressing Myself On Purpose © 2021

Black on Purpose © 2006/ 2012

When the Spirit Speaks to Me © 2012

Lord Why Did You Make Me Black ©1994/ 2009

Words of Nia © 1998

Brand New Flavor © 1992

Nia's In Love © 1992

Poems of Nia ©1990

Introducing Sister Lucy © 1990

All for You (Fiction) © 2002

CD: Black on Purpose © 2006

African Symbols and Definitions

Prepared by: Follow-pics.com

This is a picture of African symbols known as Adinkra; which are used extensively in fabrics, pottery, logos and advertising. They are incorporated into walls and other architectural features. These signs **are**

omnipresent in Ghana located in West African country on the Atlantic

Notes

CPSIA information can be obtained
at www.ICGtesting.com
Printed in the USA
LVHW091632130423
744289LV00003B/320